BORDER SOUNDS
Poems & Dispatches
From Other Timezones

BORDER SOUNDS
Poems & Dispatches
From Other Timezones

by

Kim Peter Kovac

Cover design by Shay Culligan
Cover art by Yevhenii Dubinko
Author photograph by Rives Collins

ISBN: 978-1-952326-69-1

Kelsay Books
502 South 1040 East, A-119
American Fork, Utah, 84003

For Stanley Kovac
(1920-1963)

For Lee Kovac
(1921-2018)

And, as always, for Deirdre

There is another world, and it is in this one.

—Paul Éluard

Acknowledgments

Deep gratitude to the editors of the journals who first published these pieces, sometimes in earlier versions and with different titles:

1947: "Jazz-Headed Angels"

After the Pause: "Howling After"

Allegro Poetry Magazine: "Woodcut Eyes"

Amaryllis Poetry: "Dress Me in Blue-green"

Ariel Chart: "Hanuman and the Hoopoe," "Riffing New Delhi," "Cape Town"

The Bookends Review: "Hiroshima"

Counterexample Poetics: "Surely Time Travel Doesn't Only Happen Once"

Crunchable: "Counting Genocide (City of Winds)"

Elsewhere Lit: "The Jailer, Later," "Writing Through Darkness," "Shinjuku Singing Café"

Eunoia Review: "Princely Tour"

First Literary Review–East: "Border Sounds," "Pink Moon"

Foreign Literary Journal: "Aramaic Wind," "Improbable Cacti," "On the Origin of Stories," "A Skeptic Reconsiders"

Glint Literary Journal: "12 Things About Robben Island . . . ," "My God"

Ink in Thirds: "Hello, Dali"

Ishaan Literary Review: "Removed in Berlin," "The Dome and the Doorway"

The Journal of Compressed Creative Arts: "Still Life with Zoloft"

The Muse, an International Journal of Poetry: "Deconstruction in Green"

Rain, Poetry, and Disaster Society: "Brushing Tiananmen: The Musical!," "Tiananmen Notebook"

Red Paint Hill Journal: "The Name of the Rain"

Sonic Boom: "Basho Fanboy"

Sukoon: "Blue Leopard," "Song of Petra," Boundary Lines"

Twisted Vine Literary Journal: "Passport Control, Baku"

Vine Leaves Literary Journal: "Cleaving the Map," "At the Spice Wallah"

Some of the haiku leading off sections were published, either alone or as part of a larger piece, in *Hedgerow, Beechwood Review, Origami Poems Project,* and *Ishaan Literary Review.*

Special thanks to the community at *The Poetry Barn,* especially Jennifer Givhan, Brenda Hammack, and Nandini Dhar, notably its Artistic Director, Lissa Kiernan, a long-time poetry mentor who also provided essential and gracious guidance and editing with this manuscript.

Ongoing gratitude to those who cheerfully ignored my caveat that "you are under no obligation to like, comment on, or even read these poems," including Paul, Karin, Tony, Lisa, Rives, Daniel, Laura, Jenny, Karen, Naomi, Yvette, and Simon.

Contents

Four

Five

Six

Seven

Eight

One

the Hakawatis
begin their stories with
"there was, there was not"

The Name of the Rain

Tell me your name, says the clear, deep water of the Red Sea,
the warm, oily water of the Dead Sea, the startling blue water
of the Mediterranean Sea.

Tell me your name, says the wind to the high plateau of the Negev
desert, the cloud to the granite cliffs of Wadi Rum, the olive tree
to the rocky soil of the orchard.

Tell me your name, says the red sand dune to the gazelle,
the honeybee, the hoopoe.

As the water cascades down her glowing skin, the young woman
whispers into the rain, *tell me your name.*

My God

My god comes from the desert
somewhere in the midst of Dead,
Red, and Mediterranean seas.

My god is an ambisexual
shapeshifter who writes right
to left, left to right, up to down.

My god created the blues
on a guitar, birthing them
deep in the desert of Mali.

My god is profound, profane,
snarky, sensitive, and dances
underneath the Hunger Moon.

My god plays word games
with Jesuits, Buddhist monks,
Daoists, Dervishes, Druids,

Hindus, Muslims, Sikhs,
Zoroastrians, and even
your all-purpose agnostic.

Six Eyes in Jerusalem

Walking through the Old City looking through glasses with a pair of physical eyes that live in front of another pair of chimerical eyes. Longing for long sight, the sextet of eyes scans the ancient smooth stones of the narrow streets and weathered limestone walls searching the textures of time in a city born in the 4th millennium BCE and holy to the three Abrahamic religions. The innermost eyes, born from a battle in the brain . . .

> *[being mine, struggling to rope bouncing thoughts, visions, and non-decisions that warp the world, using each other as punching bags, all the while imagining the brown recluse spider, which, just like me, has six eyes, only in three up-and-down pairs, not side by side]*

. . . begin to see the sounds of this emotionally noisy city before they are heard—a mixtape of the complicated, connected, and combative atmosphere forming a permanent shape-shifting fog.

Vodka Blessing

Ranging from un- to semi- conscious,
lying in a medical bed, nerve
synapses unable to power muscle
fibers while ghost synapses reach
back to gather and slide ahead
to the doorway at her thin place.
Deep wounds from many years
back inflicted in the name of religion
still fester brightly while we, two-thirds
of her grown-up children, with non-
specific spiritual non-dogmas, wait,
worry, wishing we knew words
and ways to speed up and ease
her inevitable crossing. Sensing
the end nearing, we decide to dab
drops of vodka (her favorite nightly
spirit) on her forehead and the cute
little flower decorating the neckline
of her nightgown, a sincerely secular
last rites. We both chuckle, knowing
she would vehemently resist even
a vaguely religious act like this.
At the same time, we remember
our youth and her imperatives to help
nurture and guide each other. This near-
final act might just be—not to trivialize—
the end of life analog to *I don't care,
eat your broccoli—it's good for you.*

I tenderly daub the good Polish vodka,
and then lick my finger for what remains
of this sacrament.

In the name of my mother, my father,
and this holy vodka.

Amen.

Boundary Lines

Just north of the Gulf of Aqaba on a stone-hot morning, the borderline hides in sandy mud between hillocks and chain links. A Syrian Serin chirps, flits, and flutters through fig branches, of course on the Jordanian side. Blurry through the air-shimmer, an Israeli Jeep cruises the beach, its Uzi-toting teenaged soldiers paying no attention to the foreign birders, one crab-stepping west toward the Israeli side, the other striding forward, right at the fence, mud-sucking as her shoes lift, step, and repeat.

The Green Line glows jagged during the first Intifada, fortunately far from the concrete-block schoolhouse on a gravel road at the edge of East Jerusalem. Children's laughter at the slapstick touring performance crackles off the walls and cement floor, stirring up dust that tastes of the desert and leaves a fine residue on the glass of sweet mint tea I've carried from the principal's office.

At the outdoor café just behind the Damascus Gate—the main entrance to the Arab Quarter of the Old City of Jerusalem—the sweet and acrid coffee is less liquid than solid. At the bottom of the cup is sludge, which leaves a damp powder on my tongue: earthy, elemental, eternal.

The House of Anxiety,

where I often dwell these days,
echoes the Church of the Holy
Sepulchre, a sprawling Jerusalem
Basilica with 30 chapels shared
by 6 sects, some say housing
the spot of the crucifixion of Jesus.

Once I was blessed with double
holy smoke: plumes from burning
incense pouring from 2 brass
thuribles taking point for duel-
ing processions of be-robed
seminarians chanting litanies.

The sounds swirl and bounce off
the stone surfaces of the church,
like the encapsulated thoughts
ricocheting in my unquiet skull.

Blue Leopard

Afternoon in Amman, April 2004, the normally teeming streets swiftly empty of civilians as soldiers wearing shades, Uzis, and mottled blue camo move into place, lurking at every intersection and rooftop. A Palestinian leader has been assassinated in the nearby West Bank, and a few hundred kilometers east, Iraq is newly roiling hot.

Next morning, calm atop Mount Nebo, gazing west reveals what the prophets saw: Jerusalem, Jericho, and the River Jordan. The tall African writer softly reveals that a young Christian from a tiny Zambian village couldn't possibly imagine ever seeing the Holy Land, especially from where Moses stood.

The writer's smooth skin is so dark it's almost midnight blue, the color of the sleek melanistic leopard that's crashed into his consciousness, slinking down the mountain while a crested honey buzzard roller-coasters above. These creatures will inhabit the poem already being written in his head.

Two

the story asks
to rest in the arms
of the story

On the Origin of Stories

The sun glints off the beryl-like blue
glacier ice mantling the Darwin Range
on *Isla Grande de Tierra del Fuego*

as I travel east in a survey boat
on the calmish waters of the Beagle
Channel *en route* to *Bahía Wulaia,*

a place sourced serendipitously
after noticing a folded paper
fallen from a field notebook

in Down House, Darwin's home.
My Master's Degree in Myth-hunting
allows access to this archived trove

of a young man's musings, jottings,
and sketches from 5 years of voyages
on the HMS Beagle. The paper

says "even the secrets have secrets,"
hand-printed under a scrawled
map locating a dome-midden left

by the Yaghan peoples who lived
eons ago. We will walk where Darwin
walked and try to dowse the soil

to stir up stories, knowing that memory
swirls the past into the future-present.
This crystal-cold and stark archipelago,

named by Europeans for the night-fires
of the indigenous folk who did not leave
writings yet surely left history and myth

here—in the air, the earth, the water,
and mostly in the memories of fires.

Cape Town

A jumble of words, languages,
dialects, accents, and, like
the all-engulfing wind
known as the "Cape Doctor,"
a dry southeaster funneling
down Table Mountain's cliffs
to sweep the city's air clean,
the voices of Africa push us all
into the future

The Jailer, Later

My gift-shop necktie is rung up
by a chatty salesclerk while waiting
for the Robben Island ferry.
He claims to have been one
of Mandela's jailers during the twenty-
seven years of imprisonment, proudly
brandishing a photo in a book, an image
bristling with clichés: one man tall, elegant,
Black, another short, pudgy, white, balding
even then. The disconnect between present
and past calls forth an Archbishop Tutu line—
God surely has a special sense of humor.

He also claims he was a friend to Mandela,
providing special privileges. While possible,
his accent is Afrikaans, the language
of power, and he was a guard in a harsh
political prison at the height of Apartheid.
I can't quite decide if he's speaking
the truth, dissembling, or just plain lying.

He must sense my doubt, continuing
his anxious monologue, but a loud-
speaker signals the ferry's departure,
so, the truth—whatever it might be—
floats, hovering between the two of us.

Still Life with Zoloft

Sun zeniths behind cloud cover
and the vibrating fog expands,
throbbing with pockets of red-
green and blue-yellow, forbidden
colors visible only when brain-
chemicals weld opposing retinal
neurons so they can't cancel out.

The air starts turning brittle,
a sound like drying glue
crackling out a percussive beat
that segues from seven-four
to a sub-Saharan polyrhythm,
conjoining the trees to ground.

The landscape looks like anxiety.

12 Things on Robben Island Not Found On Your Standard-Issue Prison Island

1. Corroded hulks of never-fired-in-anger gun batteries for Cape Town's defense during WWII.
2. A late 19th century primary school.
3. Colonies of African penguins, also known as jackass penguins because of their loud, donkey-like bray.
4. The rusting skeleton of *Fong Chung II,* a Taiwanese tuna boat impaled on rocks.
5. Fence posts made of WWII shell casings.
6. Remnants of a leper community: cemetery, church, and swimming pool.
7. The *Moturu Kramat* shrine built during Apartheid to commemorate one of Cape Town's first Imams, exiled in the 18th century.
8. Four flavors of quarries: slate, fieldstone, granite, limestone.
9. Still-running former school busses that once transported prisoners and now transport tourists.
10. Ostriches.
11. A coat of arms for the maximum-security B-section, where Mandela was imprisoned: crossed keys, books and the scales of justice. Balanced.
12. The "Cape Doctor" wind from the southeast, named for the local belief that this dry wind clears nearby Cape Town of pollution.

Writing Through Darkness

For Athol Fugard and Antjie Krog

Gratitude is too small a term
for the momentary glimpses
into the heart of your wondrous

and wounded country. Words
like "the voices of the land
all baptized in syllables

of blood and belonging,"
take life when illuminating
for those outside and afar,

allowing a slant of perception
and complex understanding
into our gaze. More moving

than the words themselves
are the acts of writing them
and speaking them aloud

and insisting they be heard.
Surely neither of you cared
you were from the tribe

of the oppressor; you wrote
hard truths and pushed them
into the limestone quarry

of the world and forced us
to look in spite of the glare.
Darkness hides behind darkness

and does not love the bright
stiletto of truth that pierces
the grief between us all.

Three

the aged tree
decides that it's time
to finally sing

Passport Control, Baku

The visa official's demeanor shrieks of a central-casting black-market smuggler. He can't find a pen, so asks—in Azeri and bad mime—if he can borrow my (favorite) pen; after he writes up the form, he pretends to forget he still has it. I have to insist several times—in English and equally bad mime—before he finally gives it back. The visa cost $185.00, US cash dollars only.

Improbable Cacti

Cactus in Baku?
Not possible.

Yet, look—
a wide cement Promenade
on the Caspian Sea -
February, wind raging
and ahead looms a
huge cactus garden.

And since it's
below freezing
the garden has become
a hundred or more
cacti wrapped
in clear plastic.

The young men showing
us around their city
are very proud
of their cactus garden,
so sweetly proud
it's not possible
to say how completely
odd this is—

growing cactus
on the Caspian
Sea.

Near the Central Station in A'dam,

my pal Susanna and I meet
to walk to *Zaal 100,* a small
jazz club. Weaving rain-lashed

tiny streets, arrival at one
hundred *Wittenstraat*—no sign,
featureless door opening
into a former school, down

narrow stairs and dim hallway,
and into a small room filled
with music-heads. mismatched
chairs, couple-three tables, drum

kit, and prone bass waiting
for plucking. We order vodka
neat and beer, respectively,
and drinks arrive in not-very-

clean glasses. Everyone knows
everyone, and Susanna, part
of Dutch avant-jazz royalty,
introduces me to Willem, Ab,

Jasper and Ig. I'm the outlander
observing talk, drinking, laughter,
quartet noodling through warm-
ups and without pause

or warning the band begins
and continues non-stop
for an hour+ lurching
from jagged to lyrical

from angular to rollicking
from atonal to dissonant
always leaving one of them
scampering.

The band, less than two
meters away engulfs my senses
with swirling fulsome music.
and just like that they

stop.

Counting Genocide (City of Winds)

Late February 2012.

In the front seat of a butch black SUV are a local driver and a translator-guide providing transportation to the airport, courtesy of the hosts of the theater festival in Baku, capital of Azerbaijan, the "Land of Fire."

The way is not smooth; this street is blocked, then that, then another—the driver curses (in Azeri probably, possibly Russian). A long line of people traverses the crosswalk in front of us, formal in dress and solemn in manner. The driver mutters and shifts (both his gears and the car's); now it's "Mr. Toad's Wild Ride"—weaving on and off sidewalks, screeching U-turns, barreling down the wrong side of the street.

The guide represents our host country—ethnically Muslim, much hospitality—and is a soothing contrast to the manic aggression of the driver. He explains the thousands of people are part of a march commemorating a tragedy 375 kilometers and 20 years away in a city called Khojaly.

- - - - -

The previous Thursday afternoon.

We're taken on a city tour, beginning with a multi-memorial park on a hill overlooking both the Caspian Sea and the incomplete gaudy theatre purpose-built for the next Eurovision singing competition. Martyr's Lane, near the entrance, honors citizens murdered when the Soviet Union collapsed two decades ago, a time known as Black January.

We speak softly near reverent locals with bright red carnations handed them by a man with hair, moustache, and suit the same shiny black to lay at the markers, horizontal like graves (probably *are* graves), photos etched on a marble wall, the lane stretching maybe a hundred meters. At the end is a tall stone monument with eternal flame and to the left and down some steps a cemetery for other national heroes—the same ground where the corpses from the 1918 Battle of Baku were removed by the Bolsheviks to turn the site into an amusement park. It was restored as a memorial following Black January.

One of the guides asks if we are moved by the graves, the line of pictures, the flame. He asks several times.

Saying *yes* is gracious, and I do. Yet I am not moved, not at all.

That evening, thoughts return to my non-reaction. Is it because there's neither a personal connection nor an easy empathetic hook? Or is it a variation on the truism attributed to Stalin, that one death is a tragedy, a million deaths merely a statistic?

- - - - -

Sunday, a few kilometers later.

The scene of the mourners at Martyr's Lane screams back into focus as the SUV accelerates onto the freeway. The earnest young man in the front seat speaks more of the significance of this day in 1992, its importance based on the slaughter of civilians fleeing Khojaly – massacred this time by Armenians, not Soviets.

What happened was a genocide, he says. *Surely it was, don't you think?*

A long silence.

- - - - -

Six weeks previously.

Our Azeri hosts, arranging for visas, ask if any in our party have Armenian ancestry or passports, and if so, they will not be allowed into Azerbaijan.

The demand is outrageous, especially when the one person with a Greek name in our group is temporarily targeted. Our trip is for art, for theater—for children, no less.

Minimal research makes plain the wounds between the Armenians and Azeris are deep and long-standing, with violence exploding after the collapse of the Soviet Union. Khojaly is merely a recent chapter—a tragedy transformed into a rhetorical cudgel in an age-old conflict over religion, power, and who can claim a patch of ground as their homeland.

- - - - -

In the SUV, the young man has not been answered.

The skeleton of the story of Khojaly is clear, but the numbers of dead are still disputed. The count ranges from 161, say the Armenians, to 613, say the Azeris. There are also accusations of ethnic cleansing and mutilation of women and children.

Still. Six hundred thirteen. Light-years fewer than the 800,000 machete-hacked by the Hutus in Rwanda, or the 6 million murdered in the Holocaust, or the 7 million force-starved in the Holodomor in Ukraine by Stalin (see above).

The question appears, electric and buzzy like neon, yet icy in its detachment: *Just how many make a genocide, anyway?*

- - - - -

We near the airport on a crisp and sunny morning with the wild Kzary wind blowing from the north over the Caspian Sea through Baku, the City of Winds, where everyone has been gracious, welcoming, and as warm as one could hope. It seems the wrong context for parsing the quantification of a horrible tragedy. Or massacre. Or genocide.

Because the earnest young man in the SUV and his countryman back at the memorial park seem to be, underneath all the nationalism, chest-thumping, and culture clash, asking the same question to a near-stranger: *Will you acknowledge our grief, name it as we do, share it just a bit?*

My (mostly non-) response is a sympathetic mumble, too stuck in a hamster-wheel of history and politics and defining intent to realize they both might have had family killed. And even if they hadn't, how would that make the murders any less senseless? These are national wounds, something we Americans came to understand on 9/11. The dead are still dead, and their families and countries grieve.

In the back of the SUV, back spasms dart up my spine—either from the hotel bed or from the disconnect between what I feel and what my empathetic depths think I should feel. It is ephemeral yet dimensional, hovering between politics and people, between clarity and cliché and impossible to reconcile because it also hovers between humanity and history.

- - - - -

44

At the airport.

As luggage is unloaded, I send thanks to all the hosts with hopes to someday, *Insha'Allah,* return. At the terminal doorway, as I turn to wave goodbye, the winter sun slants and the Kzary gusts hard and clean.

Border Sounds

waking
in the hurt
country
after
border cross
at dusk.
the past
has its own
sound –
pulsing,
trilling,
murmuring
beyond.

Four

our stories ride
with us as we walk
through our days.

East Berlin (1986)

How can a city of a million+
be so unearthly quiet? Filling
ears: a grey-green silence.

Deconstruction in Green

At astronomical dawn, when the night sky
turns barely not-black, behind each building
is a spirit-structure which did not survive
the bombs and tanks, bazookas and troops,
seen only as a structural outline in light—
a yellow-green transparent shimmer, a glow

limning a once-pulsing edifice that wills
itself to not be buried and forgotten.
As babies boomed after the war
so buildings exploded into being
in Warsaw, Berlin, London, Tokyo, more,
most clothed in oh-so-postwar concrete,

quick-drying for quick reconstruction,
mixed to obliterate memory of destruction.
Plain and practical buildings birthed
from the rubble, like children, pulse anew
with the foresight to see the past clearly
divining the green outlines of former lives.

Surely Time Travel Doesn't Only Happen Once

Flash back to the twenty-fifth of February,1979, after dark, a field
on a ridge filling with a gallimaufry of cars, vans, and pickups
parking randomly. Some stars are visible as well as lambent light
from a pink moon painting ripples on the Columbia River just
below.

As dawn reveals a socked-in morning a raggedy-ass group slowly
creaks awake—a couple-odd hundred students, astronomy nerds,
thrill-seekers, and a passel of neo-Druids in monkish robes too late
for the full-blown sacred ritual at the full-size concrete
reproduction of Stonehenge just to the north.

We're near tiny Maryhill, Washington, where there is a faux-henge
with axis aligned astronomically, right where the news predicts a
high chance of clear sky and seeing a total eclipse of the sun.

Winter, windy, warmth from banged-up thermoses of coffee,
chased with cigarettes, a few tabs of Orange Sunshine painting the
eye-whites of acid-heads here and there. Semi-unity comes from
related rituals—watching watches and cloud-cover and the refrain
hey, dude, think we'll see the 'clipse?

as if conducted, conversation ceases and everyone pivots east,
facing the bright glow of the hidden sun—chanting and whispering
to their preferred god or pharmacology to let cliché become
manifest and open the sky.

With only seconds to spare—*the sun!*—and instantly, the moon
starts eating it. As brightness fades, sound brightens: a shrill
rattling thrum like a gazillion just-hatched cicadas, louder and
louder until the black moon moves full over the sun and all the
light is instantly

suckedoutofthesky.

In unplanned unison, everyone starts screeching with triumphant joy, leaping about the bumpy field, with the only stillness/silence from the neo-Druids staring calmly at the eclipsed sun. I am nearby, and their interconnected breath reaches out and grabs mine. In a flash, we're surrounded by dry-stone dwellings with rounded roofs, gravestones, embraced by a sage, primeval wind, swirling around the seventh-century monastery on Skellig Michael off the coast of County Kerry.

There are no monks save us, but we are *there*.

A half-minute (half-day?) later, the darkness ends, and sunlight reveals cars, field, and river.

That evening, trying to ratchet back my cynicism to parse the spine of *how could this happen?* with no internal chemical alteration. Is it possible the accumulated beliefs of the bearded and be-robed near the clone-henge during the eclipse dragged me with them to another time and space?

Or maybe alchemy was at work, since it never happened again, despite mixing all the parts, factors, and elements. Even the pink moon.

Hello, Dali

—Take me, I am the drug
　　　—Salvador Dali

The pharma invitation
is the opening song
to the musical "Hello, Dali".

Eat Me, sang Alice, disguised
as a tab of Purple Haze
not grape-flavored, more tart

with that metallic backsplash,
the sure sign the acid's been cut
with speed, thus, awake all night

writing surrealistic show tunes.

Howling After

In the roaring winter dusk,
the ghostly clothes of jazz,
as heavy as the moon, dance
under the battered bridge

listening to the terror
of wartime—crazy time,
animal soup of time.
Heartless horrors, waking

nightmares illuminated
in supernatural darkness
by the flashing alchemy
of the trembling cosmos.

Removed in Berlin

On Berlin streets pursuing the removed,
rambling this crisp, clean city—
trying to sense the buried memories.

Walking what was once East Berlin,
the oppressive grey of that era
still washing streets and psyches.

The Stasi museum displays spy-toys,
dances around death, informant betrayal
and secret police in uniforms (and not).

The *Fuehrerbunker,* where Adolph and Eva
committed suicide at the end of the war,
is now under a parking lot, just steps

from the Holocaust Memorial—called,
with quintessential German directness,
"Memorial to the Murdered Jews of Europe".

This area was the administrative locus
of the national socialist murder machine,
and in its midst, the memorial, a forest

of 3,000+ pillars, all different heights,
cobbled paths between, sloping downwards
toward the center, consciously disorienting.

Underground info center, a virtual
museum including the "Room of Names,"
a curated theater of remembrance:

names of some of the murdered,
words in light projected onto all four walls,
and underneath: birth and death-dates.

Simultaneously, from speakers:
German language stories, linked
to the names, roiling eyes and ears.

Hannah, Treblinka, Mutter, Warsaw,
Lev, Sobibor, Zyklon B gas, Jakob,
neun jahre alt, rabbi, transport

Yakof,
tot,
Yheil,
tot,
Yosi,
tot,
Yerukhim,
tot,
Yitskhot,
tot,
Yosef,
tot,
Yekusie,
tot,
Yigah,
tot

Aaron,
tot,
ZviOtto,
tot.

The droning parched voice doubles
and redoubles, segues into chant
and *bang,* the bottom drops out.

Abstract shadows and statistics
now tangible and throbbing,
tasting the spirit of young ZviOtto.

Exit by way of an elevator,
outside into the air and sun,
a long breath, and another,

and another.

Five

the story asks
to take a ride
in the story

Riffing on Delhi

As oppressive as smog
is the traffic soundscape
floating over other noises
in this noisiest of cities.
It's a lyrical racket,
like Phil Glass & Ornette
jamming with a fluid street
band: thrumming bus engines,
percussive brake-squeals,
the chatter of tuk-tuk
motors and a chorus
of car horns, singing
alone and together,
like the voices of more
people than seem possible,
pulsing the city's arteries.

A Skeptic Reconsiders

In India, 23 million Sikhs worship one god, 31 million Christians worship one god, 190 million Muslims worship one god, and over a billion Hindus worship thirty-three million gods for a grand total of thirty-three million and three gods.

Astonishing

Princely Tour

The charm-biscuit guide overflows
with history, culture, and religion,

and the route includes sites important
to Hindus, Muslims, Sikhs, Baha'i,

architecture buffs, political geeks,
and enthusiasts of all the arts.

The tour samples the sacred and secular
stew that has always epitomized Delhi,

filled with great peoples, societies, & faiths
at their most glorious and violent.

A compliment about his silver bangle
brings the revelation that it's a symbol

of his status as a Brahmin prince
with personal devotion to Krishna,

possibly the reason for visiting the temple
of the "Society of Krishna Consciousness,"

featuring a trip through an animatronic
multimedia show on the *Ramayana*

and *Mahabharata*—India's history
in twenty-three over-the-top minutes.

It's easy for an outlander to be skeptical
about a guide-for-hire being a prince,

yet at day's end, while waving goodbye,
the sun catches his bracelet, momentarily

reflecting a light-shaft in the same vibrant blue
as the skin on the temple's Krishna statue.

Word-Flashlight

Stored in the basement of my brain
are stacks of boxes filled with words—
some dusty from long stays,
some still fresh with Sharpie
scrawls detailing what's inside.

Writing this poem, I tear
open box after box
seeking the right word
or phrase to complete blank
moments in the thought-stream.

This storehouse is growing
in size—the bespoke cocktail
of psychotropic meds helps
level lurching moods, but not
the articulation of them.
The stutter-step movement

of words halts after
the word-finding flashlight
swirls frantically yet fails
to illuminate voice.

Cleaving the Map

A note of comparative calm in the gigantic
Delhi book fair is the panel on storytelling,
fiction, and theater for children and young
people, where I share the small stage

with a voluble, erudite male scholar
and a warm, bubbly woman who
writes and illustrates picture books.
While drinking tea afterward, a casual

question about upcoming Indian elections
elicits immediate flashing rage, simmering
since the 1947 Partition, which even outsiders
know was filled with disruption, destruction,

and death. *"Brit colonialists,"* she spits,
*carved the country with cleavers, ignorant
and arrogant: splitting Punjab and Bengal
right through their spines.* The wounds

to families, cities, religions—and herself—
still, ooze bright and wet, splashing festered
pain on the current campaign and our teacups.
She then tucks away her short rant,

reaches into her backpack and gifts
me a copy of her newest book—
stories of fantastical adventures—
to take home to my young daughter.

At the Spice Wallah

long pepper
black salt
holy basil

Hanuman and the Hoopoe

Monkey-god Hanuman hangs out
on my shoulder since descending
from a tree as I crossed a dusty
and stupid-busy street very close
to the Red Fort in Old Delhi years
ago. These days he's confused
at the pinfeathers emerging
from my fingertips, growing since
the wind chanting Akkadian
words swirled overhead
mimicking the soaring Hoopoe
born on a sandstone cliff
on the Zagros Mountains,
near where language began.

Six

stories gliding
from the jagged clifftops—
kites on the wind

Pink Moon

During the night of the pink moon, the shadow
of the sun swims in front of the light. Crescent
gulps turn the lunar disk black, terrifying
the cicadas into stone-cold silence.

Brushing Tiananmen: The Musical!

Travel Dispatch Productions in association with
Theatre of the Reddish Star presents
Brushing Tiananmen: The Musical!

Book and lyrics by Kim Peter Kovac

Music by Bright Sheng & the Chinese Dub Orchestra

Production Design
Ai Weiwei & Communist Monument Associates

Costume Design
Knockoff Enterprises &Thunder Armour

Lighting Design
Beijing Smog, Inc.

Sound Design
Spotify

Hair/Wig Design
Humidity, Drizzle, & Co.

Music direction
Buck S. Pearl

Director and Choreographer
SunTzu

Brushing Tiananmen is made possible through the generosity of
the Cold Mountain Musical Theater Fund

Major support is provided also provided by
Red Fox Brush Company
Obscure Large City University
College of Visual Arts and Commerce

CAST OF CHARACTERS

(In Order of Appearance)

GUS...Kim Peter Kovac

LI PO..Duo Duo

GIRL .... Miahua Huang

BOY...Zhi Peng

TANK MAN...Wang Wei

PAINTER..Chay Wang

ART PROFESSOR..Xu Guan

The Ensemble plays kite-flying families, students, shoppers, pedestrians, police, and boatmen.

MUSICAL NUMBERS

ACT I

Overture...Orchestra

PROLOGUE: A BOAT SAILING THE THREE GORGES OF THE YANGTZE, 2002

Reading Li Po on Deck.......................................Gus

Kites on the Wild Yangtze.....................Li Po, Ensemble

SCENE 1: A PEDESTRIAN TUNNEL

Under Chang-An Avenue...Gus

SCENE 2: TIANANMEN SQUARE

Bigger than I Imagined and SO Communist......................Gus

Flying Kites on a Sunday Afternoon ....Ensemble

SCENE 3: CHANG'AN AVENUE (THREE YEARS
PREVIOUS, 1999)

A Convoy of Tanks and Me...................Tank Man, Ensemble

March to Prison Dance...............Police, Student Demonstrators

SCENE 4: TIANANMEN SQUARE (THE PRESENT, 2002)

Trying to Honor a Brave and Honorable Man.................Gus

Hi, American, Can We Walk & Practice English?.....Girl, Boy

SCENE 5: THE FORBIDDEN CITY (AN HOUR PREVIOUS)

Scholarship Paintings for Sale Dance.............Girl, Ensemble

We Have to Pee, the Line's Too Long,
Charge the Men's Room & Sing our Song......Women's Chorus

SCENE 6: TIANANMEN SQUARE (THE PRESENT)

Want to See Some Paintings, Proceeds to Scholarships?.....Girl

I'm Being Hustled, but It's Okay ....Gus

74

INTERMISSION

(Beer, wine, green tea, shrimp crackers,
People's Liberation Army Red Star Hats,
and brush paintings for sale in the lobby)

ACT II

SCENE 1: WINDING THROUGH THE HUTONGS

Song of Adventure and Fear................…..……….Company

SCENE 2: A SMALL ROOM OFF A DARK COURTYARD

It is Such an Honor:
Please Study the Paintings.................…..…Girl, Painter, Professor

Medley: On the Painting is Li Po/
Is It Truly Li Po?...Girl, Gus

Bargaining Dance...............Gus, Painter, Professor, Ensemble

SCENE 3: THE HUTONG OF SOUVENIRS

Medley: I'll Walk You Back/You Don't Need To........Girl, Gus

Goodbye, I Hope You Like Your Painting.................…..……Girl

SCENE 4: APPROACHING THE ARROW TOWER

I Didn't get Mugged, I'm like a Phoenix....................…..Gus

SCENE 5: TIANANMEN SQUARE

Tank Man, Brave and Proud.............Gus, Ensemble in disguise

EPILOGUE: A CLUTTERED BASEMENT ROOM IN THE USA
(TEN YEARS LATER)

It's Me on the Painting,
Time to Start Writing Poetry, Gus..........................Li Po

Meet the Performers

Kim Peter Kovac (Gus) is thrilled to be appearing in Tiananmen Square for the first time. He has appeared in the film "The Pelican Brief" and most of his stage roles in musicals for young audiences are playing "the white guy". He's a hipster-wannabe living in Portland, Oregon because he can't afford Brooklyn.

Duo Duo (Li Po) is a poet who is honored to be playing an 8th century T'ang Dynasty poet, one of the "big three", with Du Fu and Wang Wei. A major proponent of the Chinese Misty Poets movement, he was also witness to the Tiananmen Square protests.

Wang Wei (Tank Man) is honored to be playing Tank Man standing on Chang'an Avenue, both because of his bravery and because Chang'an was the capital city during the T'ang Dynasty when he wrote. He is pleased that for this role he can wear slacks and a white shirt instead of his usual robes.

Miahua Huang (Girl) hopes someday to either be a clothing designer or a translator. She regrets not being the translator for Mike Daisey's "The Agony and Ecstasy of Steve Jobs", because then she would have been on "This American Life".

Zhi Peng (Boy), studied Ballet at the State Ballet Company and Hip-Hop on the streets of Shanghai. He is thrilled to be appearing in this musical with Miahua Huang and hopes they will soon be appearing together on a dinner date.

Chay Wang (Painter) is a seventh-generation brush painter and calligrapher who teaches beginning, intermediate, and advanced brush painting as well as calligraphy at the Obscure Large City University department of Visual and Obfuscation Arts. This is his first musical.

76

Xu Guan (Professor) is emperor of the Department of Visual and Obfuscation Arts at Obscure Large City University and a former Art Director for Bruce Lee movies. As a true believer in nepotism, he is honored to be the uncle of actress Miahua Huang.

Qutang, Wu, & Xiling

are, in downstream order,
the 3 Gorges of the Yangtze,
known locally as "windbox gorge",
"witches gorge", & "death passage".
Sailing them in a colonial-
era tourist boat solidified
my deep new poet-crush
on Li Po, one of the T'ang
Dynasty's Big 3, who brush-
wrote of "pale half-moon-
light floating, before plunging
through the Yangtze gorges
with immense eastward-flowing
water". Even filtered through
12 and a half centuries
and an imperfect (like all)
translation, the heart
thrills and the pen bows
in admiration and honor.

Tiananmen Notebook

1. Near the exit from Beijing's Forbidden City, a lucky traveler standing at a men's room urinal can delight in the invasion of a gaggle of giggling women tired of waiting in line for the women's room.
2. Walk through the Tiananmen Gate toward the square of the same name and turn 180 degrees after twenty paces. You'll then fully experience the full impact of the 5 meters x 7 meters painting of Chairman Mao over the gateway.
3. Between the gate and the square lies Chang'an Avenue—one of Beijing's main drags, ten lanes wide, no crosswalks in sight, a gazillion cars and a quarter-gazillion bicycles.
4. The resourceful newbie should eventually stumble on a poorly marked crumbly staircase leading to a tunnel under the road.
5. At the other end of the tunnel and up even more crumbly concrete stairs the square is bustling with families, food vendors, and kite fliers.
6. Big is too small a word for Tiananmen Square—it's the area of a hundred football fields. On the east sideline is the National Museum of China, on the west is the Great Hall of the People, both built to scale. Oh, and Mao's Mausoleum: imagine the Lincoln Memorial tarted up with overdone classic Chinese architectural forms.
7. Experiencing the square with its ultra-uber-communist architecture will create a psychedelic perceptual disconnect after the traditional Chinese palatial architecture of the 9,800+ room Forbidden City complex.
8. The Chang'an Avenue you just crossed under is the site of the iconic (Western) image of the 1989 Tiananmen Square Protests: a thin young man in black slacks, white shirt, and shopping bags standing down a line of tanks.
9. We don't really know who he was—was being the operative word, as he has disappeared. Or *was* disappeared.

10. If fortune smiled on him, he's in hiding. If not, he's dead. It is sadly appropriate that he is known to the world at large only as "Tank Man".
11. The cloying cloak of August humidity is topped only by the low percentage of oxygen in the smogosphere.
12. A tourist wishing to honor Tank Man can stand in the square with two shopping bags looking a few blocks east down Chang'An avenue. (Standing on the avenue itself will only get you run over by cars, bicycles, or both.)
13. However, during your vigil, be prepared for interruptions by student-types whose opening gambit to elicit a *can I practice my English?* conversation is asking *are you lost?*
14. Questions about long-ago history like the Arrow Tower are answered; questions about recent history are treated as if you were speaking Urdu.
15. The offer to be guided to brush paintings being sold for art-student scholarships is a hustle, since the same offer was made at several out of the way buildings in the Forbidden City.
16. In this particular hustle, *just a few minutes' walk* means thirty-eight minutes, through the maze-like unmarked alleys of the Dazhalen hutong, filled with crowded traditional interconnected courtyard dwellings. Leaving breadcrumbs would not have been a bad idea.
17. Since imitation is a virtue in brush paintings, a lot of them look pretty similar. Drinking tea and careful examination are polite (read: expected) and words like "honored" will go a long way with the older gentleman who is (of course) in charge.
18. Mentioning love of the great T'ang Dynasty poets Du Fu and Li Po (AKA Tu Fu and Li Bai) will score points with students and professor; reading much admired poetry before a visit to another country can help open a tiny door to understanding a culture.

19. Though it's surely part of the hustle, a painting that includes a man in a robe near water with some words in Chinese could actually be Li Po, since legend has it that he, while drunk, drowned in a lake while reaching for the image of the moon in the water.
20. Post-purchase, it can take time to convince the young woman who is the chief translator that guidance back to the square is not necessary. Transaction already complete, her offer is not a hustle, but gracious.
21. Remember to carry the card from the hotel that has the name of said hotel and a dozen tourist attractions in both Mandarin and English.
22. Sleeping on the square is undoubtedly forbidden, though it would be fun to imitate the Madame Tussaud-like "Great Helmsman" lying in his crystal casket.

Seven

the pond holds
the creek by the hand—
mother and child

Dress Me in Blue-green

Dress me in blue-
green, the color
of the verge now

in focus ahead—
a border formed
between present

life and next, half-
life, built from frag-
ments of radium

heat pulsing out-
ward, radiance
thrumming on sign-

posts ahead. Dress
me in blue-green,
please; I'm on the verge.

Hiroshima

Archeologists exploring the ruined city discover a ruined statue of a young girl holding a ruined steel origami crane over her head near images of people burned into battered concrete. Words on the broken stone below the broken girl: *This is our cry; this is our prayer. Peace.*

Basho Fanboy

I had no idea how much this persona had spread until I run into a group of Tokyo university drama students in Copenhagen. Knowing only English, my transcription of the intro by the professor:

Japanese words, Japanese words, Japanese words, Japanese words, Japanese words, KIM-SAN, Japanese words, Japanese words, Japanese words, Japanese words, Japanese words, Japanese words, Japanese words, BASHO, Japanese words, Japanese words, Japanese words.

All of us smile and bow politely.

Woodcut Eyes

stare out from a narrow
woodblock print hung
in a small gallery full
of Japanese ghosts,
ogres, and demons.

The eyes of "Shoki
the Demon Queller"
stab out so sharply
that spooked & scared
travelling outlanders
understand exactly
where to go to have
their demons quelled.

Jazz-Headed Angels

Listening to jazz at dawn:
a joyride illuminating
broken hearts, a kind light
from a whispering ancient
moon, radiant with floating
angel-headed children.

Shinjuku Singing Café

An experience that pings the heights
of sweetness and strangeness at once:
an evening in a Tokyo "singing café",

a relic of some decades past,
where young radicals gathered
with lyric books & liquor

to sing largely protest songs.
The current incarnation, upstairs
in a surprisingly quiet Shinjuku

side-street, is lubricated less by booze
& politics than music & fellowship—
a decidedly non-Karaoke ambiance.

Ducking back after a quick smoke
in the stairwell, I am ambushed
and dragged onstage by my Aussie

partners-in-crime, forcing me
to sing, of all possible choices,
"Edelweiss" from "Sound of Music".

The explanation, probably:
it's not uncommon for some
folk whose mother tongue

is not English, in a gathering
where the lingua Franca,
(as it were) is English, to call

Australia Austria and vice-versa.
A tribute to a down-under flower
must have been the pianist's choice,

belying my Viennese pal
who once said *I'm from Austria.*
Austria, the one NOT with kangas.

The middle-aged audience
of gracious Japanese applauds
our amateur efforts enthusiastically,

and we are (thank God) followed
by our operatic baritone host singing
"Old Man River" in his mother tongue,

a loving interpretation, transforming
our river into an even more mythic one
sourced on the slopes of Fuji-san.

Eight

Kafka writes
stories on his phone,
posts them on Insta

Travel Insurance on Neck-Chains

1. St. Jude medal (patron saint of impossible causes).
2. Black enameled medic-alert badge in the shape of a small military dog-tag.
3. St. (Mr.?) Christopher medal (patron saint of travelers)—still worshipped but removed from the Catholic Canon of Saints due to lack of evidence that he existed.
4. St. Genesius medal (patron saint of actors, lawyers, and clowns).
5. Medal-sized replica of "The Mouth of Truth", a tall Roman stone disc carved with a humanoid face, holes for eyes, a gaping mouth. The legend states that if you put your hand in the mouth and tell a lie, it will bite it off. (Not true, I tried).
6. Silver medal with my name in Arabic.
7. Metal capsule with small pills. When questioned by airport security, I never call them Nitroglycerine, which they are, only "heart meds".

The Myth-Hunter and the Seven Mysteries

I.

Deep in the dark, dangerous forest
called *Silva Nigra* by Imperial Romans
lives Erdmann Cave, named for dwarves
that dwell there, the *Erdmännchen,*
a word that also means Meerkat,
creatures native to African grasslands,
not normally found in a famous German
forest of oak, beech, and fir trees dark-hued
enough to have been christened "black."

No dwarves (or Meerkats) in sight,
I drift away from chattery tourists,
sneaking back to search beyond
a giant stalactite for an oval lime-
stone hollow 12 meters north of it.

And here it is—a fragment of red—
terra sigillata pottery embedded in rock.
I can see the word *septem* and a bas-
relief of a man being born from a rock—
definitely Mithraic iconography.

II.

A ginger-haired Irish Dominican
monk wields a lyrical brogue as he
shepherds guests through the 11th
century basilica of Rome's *San Clemente.*

A fistful of lira into the donation box
grants a personal tour. I am led
down two damp, sweaty flights

of granite steps past the fourth
century basilica. The monk's voice
quivers with conspiratorial excitement
as he leads down to a Temple of Mithras,
a god worshipped by soldiers, birthed
from the Persian Zoroastrian religion.

Even bathed in blue light, the stark
and angular chamber is filled
with ancient memories of the rituals
of the seven mysteries, with the rough
rock ceiling doming the Alta stone.

The quest leads to the nearby Mithraic
schoolroom, warmer in feel and more
relaxed, chockablock with Amphora,
pottery and some aged paintings
on stone benches. I can make out
mountains and the Latin words *alba*
(white) and *elficidium* (dwarf).

III.

The foothills of the Zagros Mountains
in eastern Persia—likely the birthplace
of the Zoroastrian religion—is a region
rich in Mulberry trees whose leaves
murmur words with ancient roots.
Chants on the breeze of *yedi, cirtdan,*
beyaz, qor help weave
threads, sounds, and meanings
into an origin-story tapestry.

IV.

The woven storyboard sketches
a puzzling maze with elusive clues—
two scholars, a forest and a group
of people wrapped in stories living
with them in a towering library.
in other stories, shapes of bouncing
letters struggling to coalesce
into words.

Me and My Spirit-Bird

Dreams of falling from cliffs,
rescued by my swooping
spirit-bird. Just as the Hoopoe
was the guide for the Persian
epic poem, "The Conference
of the Birds", could he perhaps
shepherd me to places where
external and internal spirits dwell,
regions occupied by God, Allah,
Buddha, Zoroaster and/or thirty-
three million Hindu gods?

The Trees of Tierra del Fuego

are children
of children
of children
of children

none of us is clever
enough to crack codes
of their language
to learn names
and songs known
since time before time

these trees sing of survival
& sacrifice & celebrate
their ancestors
who lost limbs, skin
& stems to the Yaghan
people chopping with axes
of stone & bone
for fires of healing
& warmth

europeans who christened
this wild and windy place
"the land of fire"
were too self-absorbed
to listen for the names
of each individual conifer,
southern beech, &
winter's bark
tree

The Dome and the Doorway

Cosmography charts the unbounded
range of what we know, think
we know, believe we know,
and might help grokking
this universe by agnostics
who are not astrophysicists
through doorways at places
like Luxor, Fuji and Uluru.

Vertical rays of the sun crash
into the horizontal plane of desert
and cretaceous karsted limestone
rock west of the River Jordan
and create a crucible of philosophy
and faith, seen in the Foundation
Stone, now within the Dome
of the Rock on Temple Mount
in the city Arabs call Al-Quds,
which others call Jerusalem.

This is where the Talmud declares
the world was created, the meld
of heaven and earth, the altar
of Abraham and Isaac where
a white horse's night journey
flew Muhammad to meet prophets
including Adam, Moses, and Jesus,
the beating heart of an inhospitable
expanse of earth that birthed three
monotheistic faiths fiercely followed
and fought over by half the planet.

Even a nearly non-believer in the shrine
of the Dome of the Rock—a still place
hovering over an emotionally loud city—
can feel the quiet, thrumming stirrings
of a venerable far-reaching empathy,
an expanding energy that encompasses
all who we are and all that we know.
Neither the Talmud, the Bible, the Koran,
nor MapQuest notes the doorway
at the Foundation Stone, yet it is seen
by all who walk with still soft-
ness through this ageless desert.

Aramaic Wind

The wind flutters the compass needle.
The wind blows under our layers, lifting.
The wind thinks and does not judge.
The heartbeat of the wind glows within.
The wind answers in an ancestral language.

Song of Petra

Winter sunset splashes cardinal colors
over an antique city carved from red
sandstone in the desert midway

between the Dead and Red seas:
Petra, now a tourist magnet, once
a vibrant capital and caravan hub.

The poet who wrote "rose-red city,
half as old as time" spent no days
there; the carved walls would say

that "rose-red" is a dull description,
and the rocks have no remembrance
of him, though they whisper tales

and secret stories of so many others
when you touch them, close your eyes
and say, *there was, there was not.*

The rock-ness of Petra belies the life
of this spirited city, with citizens guided
and guarded by pre-Islamic Arab gods,

later a home to revolutionaries
fighting with white-robed Lawrence.
After climbing the steep, winding path

to the highest carved building,
the Monastery, whispering rocks
chant other legends as prayers.

The Bedouin families living in caves
carved into *Jebel al-Madhbah,*
the mountain of the altar, can trace

their ancestry farther back than history.
The rocks look like them, and they
like the rocks: stunning and steely,

and the poetry of their faces calls out
in a language before language,
in words before words, and you hear

deep inside you a lucid, liminal
song, swirling through the mountains
of this vernal city older than time.

Notes

One
Hakawati is the Arabic word for "storyteller".

My God
This owes a debt to Sandra Beasley's poem of the same name.

Vodka Blessing
For my mother, Lee.

The House of Anxiety
Catholics believe the location of the crucifixion is within this church, called Calvary (from Latin) or Golgotha (from Aramaic), both meaning "the place of the skull." If you walk up a circular stairway & kneel under the altar you can reach your hand through a silver disc enclosing a hole in the floor and touch the rock.

Blue Leopard
A black panther is the melanistic color variant of any big cat species, and black panthers in Africa are leopards. A blue leopard does not actually exist in nature.

On the Origin of Stories
For Freddie and Myrna Gershon.

Border Sounds
"The past has its own sound" is borrowed from Laura Schellhardt's play *Digging Up Dessa.*

Hello, Dali
The title of Jimi Hendrix's "Purple Haze" is said to have been inspired by the name of a batch of LSD delivered to the 1967 Monterey Pop Festival by pioneering sound engineer and LSD mega-manufacturer Owsley Stanley.

Surely Time Travel Doesn't Only Happen Once
3.6 million tabs of LSD (AKA acid) under the name Orange
Sunshine were distributed from a lab in Sonoma County California.

Writing Through Darkness
The epigraph references playwright/director/actor Athol Fugard and
poet/journalist Antjie Krog, South African writers (of Afrikaans
descent) during and after Apartheid. The internal quotation is from
Krog's poem "Country of Grief and Grace".

Howling After and **Jazz-Headed Angels**
Both are erasure poems, remixed from Allen Ginsburg's "Howl".

Song of Petra
"Rose-red city half as old as time" is the end of "Petra", by John
William Burgon, written in 1845. "There was, there was not" is a
traditional beginning to Arab stories, analogous to "once upon a
time." "White-robed Lawrence" refers to T.E. Lawrence, AKA
Lawrence of Arabia.

About the Author

Travel, both personal and business, has inspired and influenced much of the writing in this book, as have theatre collaborations with national and global artists.

Kim Peter Kovac has had poetry, prose poetry, flash fiction, haiku, haibun, and creative non-fiction published in journals from Australia, Bangladesh, England, India, Ireland, Korea, Poland, Scotland, Singapore, South Africa, UAE, and the USA, including *Sukoon, Frogpond, Mudlark, Ishaan Literary Review* and *The Journal of Compressed Creative Arts*.

He commissioned and produced 100+ new plays and musicals for young audiences as Artistic Director of Kennedy Center Theater for Young Audiences. He and Deirdre Kelly Lavrakas are founding co-directors of the ground-breaking play development program *New Visions/New Voices* and co-edited *New Visions/New Voices: 25 Years/25 Plays* (Dramatic Publishing, 2016).

He lives in Alexandria, Virginia.

Kelsay Books

www.ingramcontent.com/pod-product-compliance
Lightning Source LLC
Chambersburg PA
CBHW070334090426
42733CB00012B/2471